SMALL GROUP SERIES

Getting a Grip

FINDING BALANCE IN YOUR DAILY LIFE

Interactions Small Group Series:

INTER*Actions*

SMALL GROUP SERIES

Getting a Grip

FINDING BALANCE IN YOUR DAILY LIFE

BILL HYBELS

WITH KEVIN & SHERRY HARNEY

WILLOW
CREEK

RESOURCES

ZondervanPublishingHouse
Grand Rapids, Michigan

A Division of HarperCollins*Publishers*

Getting a Grip
Copyright © 1998 by the Willow Creek Association

Requests for information should be addressed to:

📖 ZondervanPublishingHouse
Grand Rapids, Michigan 49530

ISBN: 0-310-22444-6

Interior design by Rick Devon

Printed in the United States of America

98 99 00 01 02 03 04 / ❖ EP/ 10 9 8 7 6 5 4 3

CONTENTS

NTERACTIONS

1992, Willow Creek Community Church, in partnership
th Zondervan Publishing House and the Willow Creek
sociation, released a curriculum for small groups entitled
e Walking with God series. In just three years, almost a half
llion copies of these small group study guides were being
ed in churches around the world. The phenomenal
ponse to this curriculum affirmed the need for relevant and
lical small group materials.

the writing of this curriculum, there are over 1,650 small
ups meeting regularly within the structure of Willow
eek Community Church. We believe this number will
rease as we continue to place a central value on small
ups. Many other churches throughout the world are grow-
in their commitment to small group ministries as well, so
need for resources is increasing.

response to this great need, the Interactions small group
ies has been developed. Willow Creek Association and
ndervan Publishing House have joined together to create a
ole new approach to small group materials. These discus-
n guides are meant to challenge group members to a deeper
el of sharing, create lines of accountability, move followers
Christ into action, and help group members become fully
oted followers of Christ.

GGESTIONS FOR INDIVIDUAL STUDY

Begin each session with prayer. Ask God to help you
understand the passage and to apply it to your life.

A good modern translation, such as the New International Version, the New American Standard Bible, or the
New Revised Standard Version, will give you the most
help. Questions in this guide are based on the New International Version.

Read and reread the passage(s). You must know what the
passage says before you can understand what it means
and how it applies to you.

Write your answers in the spaces provided in the study
guide. This will help you to express clearly your understanding of the passage.

Keep a Bible dictionary handy. Use it to look up unfamil-
iar words, names, or places.

SUGGESTIONS FOR GROUP STUDY

1. Come to the session prepared. Careful preparation will greatly enrich your time in group discussion.
2. Be willing to join in the discussion. The leader of the group will not be lecturing but will encourage people to discuss what they have learned in the passage. Plan to share what God has taught you in your individual stud
3. Stick to the passage being studied. Base your answers c the verses being discussed rather than on outside authc ities such as commentaries or your favorite author or speaker.
4. Try to be sensitive to the other members of the group. Listen attentively when they speak, and be affirming whenever you can. This will encourage more hesitant members of the group to participate.
5. Be careful not to dominate the discussion. By all means participate, but allow others to have equal time.
6. If you are the discussion leader, you will find additiona suggestions and helpful ideas in the Leader's Notes.

ADDITIONAL RESOURCES AND TEACHING MATERIAL

At the end of this study guide you will find a collection of resources and teaching materials to help you in your growt as a follower of Christ. You will also find resources that wil help your church develop and build fully devoted follower Christ.

INTRODUCTION:
FINDING BALANCE
IN YOUR DAILY LIFE

Imagine you are behind the wheel of your car driving 45 mph on a curving mountain road. Your speed is safe for the road conditions . . . or so you think. The pavement is wet due to a light rain and, though you are not aware of it, the temperature is dropping rapidly. It is late at night and you have been driving for hours. The radio is on and your mind is focused on the road ahead of you. All of a sudden, the road feels different. The steering wheel is loose and unresponsive. Your heart begins to race as you realize the back end of your car is sliding. The rain has frozen and become a layer of ice. You are beginning to slide out of control. Reflexively, you push your foot on the brake. That action simply increases the speed you are sliding and you go into a full spin . . . you are out of control!

Your mind is racing. You are thinking, *How am I going to get out of this one? What if I don't get out of this one?* As the car spins you wonder if you will run into the trees or maybe even off the edge of the road. *Will I hit another car? Are my premiums paid?* In a fraction of a second, you wonder if you will live to tell others about this experience.

Few people ever choose to experience the feeling of being absolutely and completely out of control. It is awful. It is unnatural, uncomfortable, and can create intense anxiety. Yet from time to time, we will all experience the sheer panic of being out of control.

Sometimes we feel this way about international affairs. We pick up a newspaper, read a magazine, or turn on the news, and see a world spinning out of control and sense a powerlessness to change the course of events. Still, as uncomfortable as international chaos makes us feel, facing turmoil in our own life can make us feel even more out of control.

All of us live with a profound need to have order established in the chaos of our lives. We long for peace in the middle of turmoil. We want to discover how we can regain control of that which seems to be slipping out of our grasp. In short, we need to get a grip on our lives.

In this series of Interactions, you will discover how you can regain control of your life. We will focus on five primary areas that tend to slide out of control easily on the ice-covered roads of life. In the first session we will look at the big picture and discover where our lives are out of control. And in the following five sessions we will learn how to get a grip on our schedules, our bodies, our finances, our devotions, and our relationships.

This may seem like an enormous undertaking. That's because it is! Yet God, the One who made the heavens and the earth, is ready to help you each step of the way. He is a God of order. He can help you get a grip on your life.

Bill Hybels

GETTING A GRIP ON YOUR LIFE

A mother stopped at her parents' home for just a few moments to pick something up. While she went into the house with her two little children, she left her car running in the driveway. As they were coming back out, her four-year-old boy ran to the car, opened the door, climbed in the driver's seat and accidentally hit the gearshift lever. He put the car into drive and it ran right through the garage door of her parents' house. The mother stood in stunned amazement as she watched the car crash through the door. There was *nothing she could do*. It was out of her control. Thankfully, no one was injured.

Not many days later the woman's husband was driving the same car. He was dropping off a friend at home and his four-year-old son was sitting in the backseat. As the father was driving up the driveway approaching his friend's garage, he realized that he was on glare ice. He put his foot on the brake but realized it wasn't going to do any good. As the car slid closer to the closed garage door, he said to his friend, "I think we're in big trouble." A moment later they crashed through the garage door.

His little boy in the backseat quietly said, "It's okay, Dad, the same thing happened to me last week."

I remember the father saying to me, "Bill, it is hard to describe how helpless I felt when I realized I was on ice and that there was nothing I could do to stop my car from crashing through my friend's garage door. It was a horrible feeling. I was utterly out of control."

1 Describe in detail a time you experienced being out of control.

overreacted to criticism

What feelings gripped your heart at that moment?

felt wronged & disrespected

Read Genesis 1:1–27

2 How do you see God creating order out of chaos in th account of creation?

*Earth was of no form
Created earth in order
by steps*

What do you learn about the character of God in this passage?

He took his time & saw the good in what he created. for us

3

Genesis 1:26 says, "Then God said, 'Let us make man in our image, in our likeness, and let them rule over the fish of the sea and the birds of the air, over the livestock, over all the earth, and over all the creatures that move along the ground.'" If human beings are created in the image of God, and God is a God of order, what do you learn about humanity from this passage?

That we need order in our life!

SHARPENING THE FOCUS

Read Snapshot "An Honest Look at Your Life"

AN HONEST LOOK AT YOUR LIFE

If you took an honest inventory of your life, you might have to admit that some things are not the way they should be. It is a rare experience to find a person who feels they have a good grip on every area of their life. Most of us struggle with feeling that parts of our life are out of control. If we portrayed our life on a pie graph and were to honestly plot each area, each of our diagrams would look different.

Look closely at a few examples of what some lives might look like:

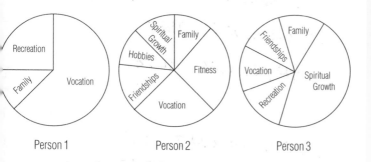

Person 1   Person 2   Person 3

4

What observations can you make about the life of *one* of the people represented above?

ONE PERSON HAS
NO SPIRITUAL GROWTH

5

Take a few minutes and create your own pie graph. Be sure it honestly reflects the levels of priority and commitment in your life. Think about where you are investing your time and energy at this time in your life. Some areas you might want to plot are: your vocation, family life, friendships, recreation, hobbies, spiritual growth, and commitment to developing physical health. Plot these and any other areas that are important to you.

What is one observation you can make about yourself by looking at your pie graph?

I SPEND ALOT MORE TIME

WORKING THAN

ANYTHING ELSE

What surprises you as you look at this representation of your life?

THE AMOUNT OF
RECREATION
TIME

6

What is one area of your life in which you feel you have a good and healthy grip?

DON'T KNOW

What is contributing to this area being so positive?

7

What area do you need to get a grip on as soon as possible?

SPIRITUAL GROWTH

What is standing in the way of you getting a grip on this area of your life?

UNCERTAINTY IN MY
CLOSEST RELATIONSHIP

What needs to change if you are going to finally get a grip on it?

WORK THRU MY
INSECURITIES

Read Snapshot "It's Time to Get a Grip"

IT'S TIME TO GET A GRIP

We live in a day and age of delayed responsibility. We hear the ads say, "Buy today and don't pay for one full year!" Credit card use is at an all-time high. We plan to start dieting and exercising "tomorrow"—but we have had these plans every day for the last year! We forget that our actions have consequences, and that *lack* of action can have just as severe consequences. Waiting, delaying, and procrastinating make change only more difficult.

It is time for us to get a grip and face reality. Postponing the battle, delaying the inevitable, and waiting until tomorrow will never make things any easier. If we are going to experience order in our chaotic lives, we need to acknowledge the disorder. We need to admit that things are spinning out of control. It's time to get a grip.

8   In the coming five sessions we will look very closely at five specific areas in which you may need to get a grip on your life. Take a moment and assess your life. On the continuum below, mark where you are right now in each area:

My Schedule

| *Spinning out of control* | *I have a loose grip on this area* | *I have a good grip on this area* |

$$1 \quad 2 \quad ③ \quad 4 \quad 5 \quad 6 \quad 7 \quad 8 \quad 9 \quad 10$$

My Physical Health

| *Spinning out of control* | *I have a loose grip on this area* | *I have a good grip on this area* |

$$1 \quad 2 \quad 3 \quad ④ \quad 5 \quad 6 \quad 7 \quad 8 \quad 9 \quad 10$$

My Personal Finances

| *Spinning out of control* | *I have a loose grip on this area* | *I have a good grip on this area* |

$$1 \quad 2 \quad 3 \quad 4 \quad 5 \quad 6 \quad 7 \quad ⑧ \quad 9 \quad 10$$

My Spiritual Growth

Spinning out of control	I have a loose grip on this area		I have a good grip on this area

1	2	3	(4)	5	6	7	8	9	10

My Relationships

Spinning out of control	I have a loose grip on this area		I have a good grip on this area

1	2	(3)	4	5	6	7	8	9	10

Identify one area of your life that your small group members can begin praying for you to grow and get a grip on in the coming weeks.

MUSIC, SCHEDULE my

LIFE

9

What is your strongest area right now?

FINANCES

How can your small group members help you celebrate the strength you are experiencing in this area of your life?

TIME INVENTORY

Take time in the coming week to take an honest assessment of how much time you spend doing the following things:

Item:	*Amount of time in a week:*
• Work and work-related activities	50 HR:
• Hobbies and recreational activities	8 HR:
• Watching TV	8 HR:
• Exercising and developing physical health	7 HR:
• Being with friends	7 HR:
• Time with your spouse (if married)	—
• Time with children (if you have them)	—
• Time reading the Bible and praying	1½
• Time in worship and with other followers of Christ	4 h:
• Other things you do:	
_____	_____
_____	_____

PERSONAL "GETTING A GRIP" LIST

When we slow down enough to really look at our lives, the chaos can feel overwhelming. So many things are out of control that we just don't know where to begin. Take time in the coming week to identify two—three at the most—areas in your life where you really desire to get a grip. Write them down below.

Areas in which I want to get a grip:

- _____ SPIRITUAL _____
- _____ MUSIC _____
- _____ READING _____

Begin praying for God to help you look honestly at each of these areas, and for strength to begin reclaiming control in each area.

GETTING A GRIP ON YOUR SCHEDULE

REFLECTIONS FROM SESSION 1

1. If you did a time inventory for yourself, what was one insight you gained about yourself and how you order your life?
2. If you formed a "Getting a Grip" list and related goals, what are you doing to get a grip on one area of your life on this list?

THE BIG PICTURE

Over the years there have been numerous "one-minute" books written. Books such as *The One Minute Manager* started it all by providing some helpful principles on managing a business. In a busy, schedule-crazed world, the book just flew off the shelves. Who wouldn't want to learn how to manage their life in just one minute?

Books to follow have been *The One Minute Lover*—I didn't bother to read that one. I have some suspicions about anyone who thinks love can be attained in sixty seconds. There is also *The One Minute Father* and *The One Minute Mother*. Can you believe it, just one minute to excellence in parenting? Seems pretty unbelievable, doesn't it?

Some years ago, when these books were really hot, I read an article called *The One Minute Christian*. The author, Greg Conelmo, with tongue in cheek, wrote about what a "one minute" book on the Christian life would look like. There could be a chapter called "The One Minute Sin." From now on, all sin, whether in word or action, should never take longer than sixty seconds. The next chapter could be "The Thirty Second Confession." If your sin only took one minute, the confession should take only half a minute. Then the next chapter could be "One Minute Repentance." Can you see how nice and neat this would be? If you have sinned the one-minute sin, you could take a minute to evaluate what you've done, how it has affected God, others, and yourself. Then, use a few seconds to ponder the temporal and eternal consequences. Finally, you could strategize how to take realistic steps to prevent your one-minute sin from occurring again.

Do you see the beauty of this? The whole process takes less than three minutes. By following these simple steps, within 180 seconds you will have experienced the agony of depravity, the cleansing of confession, and the joy of restoration. Wouldn't it be wonderful?

If people enjoyed the simplicity and convenience of these chapters, they could read on and learn about "One Minute Devotions," "One Minute Praying," "One Minute Fellowship," "One Minute Patience," and the list of chapters could go on and on. By using the dynamic new principals set forth in this book, it would take only ten minutes a day to live the Christian life.

A WIDE ANGLE VIEW

1 "One minute" books have been very popular. Why do you think so many people are attracted to this approach to life?

ITʻS A FAST FIX

WE WANT IT NOW

What is wrong with the "one-minute" approach to the Christian life described above?

Read Ecclesiastes 3:1–13 and Ephesians 5:15–20

2 What do you learn about time and scheduling from Ecclesiastes 3:1–13?

There needs to be balance

3 The apostle Paul gives great wisdom in Ephesians 5:15–20 about how we use our precious resource of time. How should we use our time?

Praising God
Wisely

How should we not use our time?

Foolishly

Summarize Paul's message in this passage in your own words. In one sentence, what is he trying to communicate?

We should consider how we live & not to waste our time Because living for the self is evil.

SHARPENING THE FOCUS

Read Snapshot "A Life Out of Balance"

A LIFE OUT OF BALANCE

Many people need to be honest and admit that there are some segments of their life that are way out of balance. They are spending too much time on things that don't matter and too little time on the things that matter most! In the community where I minister, a large number of people have way too much of their lives devoted to vocational pursuits. Some people invest excessive time in recreational pursuits. Others are so consumed with personal advancement that they have no time for family, friendship, and their spiritual life. Still others get so overcommitted at church that they are out of balance and need to step back from some of their service commitments. If your life is out of balance, it is time to be honest and begin to get a grip on your schedule.

4

To what area of your life are you devoting too much time? (You may want to refer back to session one, question five.)

Watching TV

What needs to happen for you to cut back in this area?

Plan other activitys. ~~book~~

5

What is one area you are neglecting?

Reading, Music.

What needs to happen for you to develop this area?

Read more, Practice.
find others to learn from.

Read Snapshot "A Life in Balance"

A LIFE IN BALANCE

Then there are those people who have been moving from being out of control to getting a grip on their schedules and coming into balance. They are tired of being out of control. They have sensed the Holy Spirit's power of self-control being infused into their life and they have been working diligently on balancing their life over a period of time.

These people have discovered that God is very concerned about every area of their lives. God designed humans to be creatures of labor. He is concerned that people are committed to excellence in the marketplace, but He meant for it to be a profession and not an obsession. God is also concerned about recreational life. Even Jesus left the sick and the hurting to go up on a mountain to rest, to be refreshed and refueled. And God is concerned about relationships too. In both family and friendships we need to invest the needed time to develop deep and healthy relationships. Along with all of this, God is concerned for our spiritual lives, with having us commit to corporate worship as well as carve out time every day to be with Him.

Relational	Physical
Vocational	Spiritual

6 See pie chart above for an example of a life with balance in relational, physical, vocational, and spiritual areas. What are some of the advantages of living with a life in balance?

We don't spend too much time in any one special area so we stay focused & refreshed

7 The picture painted above looks pretty balanced and positive. Can you see any problems with it?

Yes since I work 8hrs or 9hrs a day theres not enough time left for equal time in other areas.

23

Read Snapshot "A Life Beyond Balance"

A LIFE BEYOND BALANCE

Picture a pie chart with its different sections, only this pie has a cross at its center. This picture captures a very significant step in the life of a follower of Christ. Instead of the spiritual dimension of life being just another activity to be balanced with work, family, and recreation, it becomes the core of every area of life.

The Bible teaches that our relationship with Jesus Christ needs to be at the very center of our life. Jesus is the all-important, ultimate priority. When this happens, you find yourself thinking about Him throughout your day. You find yourself praying and talking to Him at your lunch hour, between conversations with other people, and while driving down the road. You spontaneously begin thinking of ways you can please Him and honor Him. You sense His presence throughout the day, and when you go for periods of time when you don't sense His presence, you say, "Oh, Lord, I'm sorry. I just went through a large portion of my day and never gave You a thought. Let's pick up from here and help me tune in to Your presence more closely." When Christ moves from just being a part of your life to become the center of it, then He will begin to influence every thought, every conversation, every decision, and every activity of your life.

8

How do you feel during those moments when you are in communication with God right in the middle of all of life's busyness?

More in control of my behavior.

What helps you stay tuned in to God's presence through the daily grind of life?

Praying

9

What is one thing you do to keep God in the center of *one* of these areas of your life:

- Your family life
- Your friendships *I mention him or*
- Your vocation
- Your free time *Praise him.*
- Some other area

10

What is one thing you need to begin doing to help you keep God in the center of *one* of these areas of your life:

- Your family life
- Your friendships
- Your vocation *— Try to do what would be*
- Your free time
- Some other area *pleasing in GODS EYES.*

If I'm not responsible then leave it be.

CHRIST IN THE CENTER

If you have identified an area of your life where Christ needs to be placed in the center, commit yourself to do all you can to make room for Him in this part of your life. First, pray for God to open this part of your life to His presence, and for God's Holy Spirit to break down any resistance you may have in surrendering this area to His control. Second, set some specific goals that will position God in the center of this area of your life (the more specific, the better). Finally, find a friend who is committed to following Christ. Ask this person to pray for you and keep you accountable. Invite that person to ask you how you are doing in this area on a weekly basis.

MAKING THE MOST OF YOUR TIME

Take time to memorize Ephesians 5:15–16:

> Be very careful, then, how you live—not as unwise but as wise, making the most of every opportunity, because the days are evil.

Pray for God to give you a deepening sense of how to use your time wisely. Pray also for eyes to see when you are using your time for things that don't have a kingdom impact.

GETTING A GRIP ON YOUR BODY

REFLECTIONS FROM SESSION 2

1. If you have been working at placing Christ at the center of a specific area of your schedule, how are you experiencing a greater sense of His presence in this area of your life?

2. If you took time to memorize Ephesians 5:15–16, would you be willing to recite it for your group? What is one way the truth of this passage has motivated you to make better use of your time?

THE BIG PICTURE

Most of us occasionally take time to set personal goals. The beginning of a new year is a natural time to set personal resolutions, but any time is a good time to honestly evaluate our lives and set goals. When we make a list of personal goals, they almost always include some mention of action to be taken with regard to our bodies.

- Take a night class toward my degree
- Work at not raising my voice with the kids
- Exercise at least three days a week
- Drop ten pounds
- Begin reading the Bible on a regular basis
- Volunteer in a ministry at church
- Take my wife out for a date on a weekly basis
- Read at least one book each month
- Stop smoking
- Run four times a week
- Start getting to bed by 11:00 P.M.

Most of us really do care about our bodies. We are concerned about how they look, how they function, and how they are maintained. However, I would guess that few of us understand how much *God* cares about our bodies. It seems we often hear about the value God puts on our souls and we forget how much He cares about our physical selves as well.

A WIDE ANGLE VIEW

1 Name one goal you have set concerning your physical health that you have kept. How has this commitment improved your quality of life?

Stair Stepping just started Stop Smoking feel Better

What is one you have not kept, and how have you regretted this?

I just stopped the exercise. Started Smoking again Disappointed!

A BIBLICAL PORTRAIT

Read Romans 12:1–2; 1 Corinthians 6:19–20

2 What does it mean to "offer our bodies as living sacrifices"?

It means to exercise + eat healthy for God + not just for ourselves

How is this an expression of worship?

By taking care of our bodies. which are temples of the Holy Spirit.

3

1 Corinthians 6:19–20 says the Holy Spirit of God actually lives within each follower of Christ. The apostle Paul reminds us of the price God paid for us (the blood of Jesus). With this in mind, we are told to "honor God with your body." What are examples of honoring God with your body?

*Getting the rest we need
Eating right
Exercising + making God
the center of these actions.*

What are examples of dishonoring God with your body?

*Eating wrong kinds of foods
Being lazy.
Having no concern of our health*

Read Snapshot "God Cares About Your Body"

GOD CARES ABOUT YOUR BODY

God cares more about our physical health and condition than we do. Our physical bodies matter to Him! God has proved this concern for our physical bodies time and time again throughout the Bible.

1. In Genesis, God molds and shapes our bodies from the dust of the earth and breathes life into them. All the rest of creation was made through His spoken word, but we were made by His hands! (Gen. 2:7)

2. Jesus taught that God provides for our physical needs. God feeds the birds and clothes the flowers. How much more will He provide for us? (Matt. 6:25–30).

3. Jesus proved the value of human bodies by taking one on Himself. He felt cold; He knew hunger; He knew pain. He also felt the embrace of a friend, the sunshine against His face, and the taste of a good meal. God chose to have His only Son come to us in a human body (Phil. 2:6–8).

4. The Holy Spirit of God dwells within each follower of Christ. In what greater way could God give dignity to our physical bodies? (1 Cor. 3:16–17).

5. God proves His concern over our bodies by promising to raise them from the dead at the end of time (1 Cor. 15:42–44; Rev. 20:5–6).

God shows us the depth of His concern for our physical bodies from Genesis to Revelation. Don't you think we should share His concern?

---

4 One way God shows His concern for your body is through providing for your needs. Finish this statement:

"God has provided for my physical well-being by ..."

My home, my job, + plenty of good food.

5 If your body is the temple (dwelling place) of the Holy Spirit, then God is always with you! If God was physically walking with you through this next week, what is one thing you would change?

I wouldn't smoke or drink alcohol.

In reality, God will be with you through every moment of the coming week (His Spirit lives in every one of His followers). Why doesn't this motivate us in the same way that His physical presence would?

Aren't as close to him — as I should be.

Read Snapshot "What You Put in Your Body"

WHAT YOU PUT IN YOUR BODY

Some years ago I used to race motorcycles with some of the guys on our church staff. We went to the track every Saturday. It was an amazing thing to watch as all the guys arrived in their beat-up vans and rickety trailers. When it came time to put fuel in the tanks of those motorcycles, these backyard grease monkeys would turn into chemists. They would take out a little jug of very high-performance fuel and then take some of the best synthetic oil on the market and would mix it together just right. Then they would take out a hankie, put it over the top of the tank, and mix it in carefully. They were meticulous about what they put in that tank; they wanted their bike at its peak performance. All this care was put into the upkeep of a thousand-dollar motorcycle.

Now think about the "fuel" we put into the priceless bodies God has given us. Look what we put into the tank of our body. We have been handmade by God, sustained by His providing hand, filled by the Holy Spirit, and given the promise of a bodily resurrection. Knowing all of this, how can we continue to put all kinds of trash into our bodies and naively assume our performance won't be affected?

6

If you compared your body to a high-power performance engine, how would you describe the fuel you are putting into it?

What needs to happen in your life and eating habits to upgrade the quality of fuel you are putting into your body?

Read Snapshot "How You Condition Your Body"

HOW YOU CONDITION YOUR BODY

The benefits of being in shape are almost too many to list. Higher energy levels, higher self-esteem, higher resistance to colds, and a controlled appetite are just a few. Doctors, and many others, praise the effects of regular exercise on the human body. I read an article some years ago by Dr. Malcom Cruthers entitled *The Emotional Healing of Running*. In this article, Cruthers communicates his belief that most people could ban the blues and fight depression with a simple, ten-minute exercise session three times a week. He continues on to say that exercise *doubles* the body's level of a particular hormone that has a long-term effect of destroying depression. With all the reports, studies, and advice that come to this same conclusion, why is it that we still struggle to condition our bodies on a regular basis?

7 What stands in the way of you developing habits of regular physical conditioning?

What can your group members do to help you develop good habits in this area?

Read Snapshot "How You Use Your Body"

HOW YOU USE YOUR BODY

You can glorify God with your body by how you use it. If Mr. Universe is not willing to be a tool in the hands of God, he becomes a tragic waste of the human body. All the years of conditioning, good eating habits, and muscle toning profit nothing if his body is not available to be used for God's purposes. You see, if all you want to be is sexier, if all you want is to be more macho, if all you want is to attract attention to yourself, you are missing the point. You need to watch what you put into your body and work at conditioning it so that you can become a tool in the hands of God. When you are in good shape—well-rested, eating good food, and taking care not to put toxic substances in your body—you can become a more energetic servant for God. You will have the strength and health to serve Him more fully.

8   What is one way you are using your physical abilities to serve God?

How would better health and a higher energy level help you in this area of service?

9   What is one goal you will set in response to the message of this session?

Helping others
Discipline to Exercise
Listen to God

Who will you ask to pray for you and hold you accountable to this new goal?

A Prayer of Confession

If you have struggled to keep a grip on your body and your physical condition, take time to pray this prayer:

Father, forgive me. Forgive me for all the "garbage" I put in my "tank." Forgive me for how I have complained about my health problems, lack of energy, and aches and pains, when often these things are a direct result of what I choose to put into my body. Forgive me for not conditioning my body the way it ought to be conditioned. My body is the temple of Your Spirit; I should treat it with dignity. Forgive me for not having the right motivation. Forgive me for not offering my body as a living sacrifice to You.

You say if I confess my sins, You are faithful to forgive and cleanse me. Today is a new day. May I experience a fresh start as I dedicate myself to glorify You with my body. I belong to You, inside and out. I matter to You, my spirit and my body. Teach me to live in a way that gives glory to You. Amen.

My Body, the Temple of God

Take time to memorize these two passages from 1 Corinthians:

Don't you know that you yourselves are God's temple and that God's Spirit lives in you? If anyone destroys God's temple, God will destroy him; for God's temple is sacred, and you are that temple.

1 Corinthians 3:16–17

Do you not know that your body is a temple of the Holy Spirit, who is in you, whom you have received from God? You are not your own; you were bought at a price. Therefore honor God with your body.

1 Corinthians 6:19–20

Prayer is putting God's name on future events. The credit goes to him not me for praying

GETTING A GRIP ON YOUR FINANCES

REFLECTIONS FROM SESSION 3

1. If you have spent time this past week confessing to God that you have put bad fuel in your physical tank or neglected conditioning your body, how has this confession empowered you to begin changing some of these habits?

2. If you have memorized 1 Corinthians 3:16–17 or 1 Corinthians 6:19–20, would you recite one of these for your group? How has the truth and conviction of these passages impacted the way you care for your body?

THE BIG PICTURE

We go to school to learn how to earn it. We work forty to sixty hours a week acquiring it. We commit Friday and Saturday evenings to creatively spending it. We get caught up for countless hours worrying if we have enough of it. We daydream about how to get even more of it. We wonder what we could do if we stumbled into a lot of it. Arguments over handling it are one of the leading causes of divorce. Despair over mishandling it has contributed significantly to the suicide rate. Love of it causes many of society's crimes. The absence of it creates some of society's greatest nightmares. Call it a root of all kinds of evil. Call it the means for supreme good. But one thing you can't do, you can't ignore it. What is it? The answer is obvious! MONEY!

Money is a very sensitive subject for many people. When the topic of personal finances comes up, tensions rise. No matter what outward appearances might indicate, this is a hot spot for many people. Some who read these words are barely making ends meet. They are working very hard but seem to be slowly sinking into a sea of debt. This creates tremendous loads of anxiety. Others have experienced the pain of financial ruin. Just talking about money and finances is like pouring salt on an open wound. Others might have a healthy income, but are still overextended and feeling the financial pinch. And there may be some who have it all together in this area and earn more income than they need. These people have most likely come to the realization that money does not guarantee happiness. The truth is, across the whole spectrum, money can be an area of real tension and struggle.

A WIDE ANGLE VIEW

1   How have you experienced tension in your life because of money?

Used to work excessively in order for to meet my family's to needs. Couldn't turn down overtime.

What is one joy you have experienced because of money?

Able to help a friend.

Read 1 Timothy 6:6–10; Proverbs 30:8–9; Hebrews 13:5

2 What are some of the possible consequences for the person who becomes consumed with a love of money?

Lose sight of God. Not being content w/what they have.

3 How should a follower of Christ view money and personal finances?

Trust God. Be content w/what you have. Check your priorities

Read Snapshot "Beware of the 'Permissible Lie'!"

BEWARE OF THE "PERMISSIBLE LIE"!

One deadly threat to our personal finances is deceitful advertising. Just think about it, there are thousands of brilliant, well-trained, highly paid professionals who are trying to find a way to motivate you to purchase their products. These professionals are competing against other advertisers who want you to purchase their products. The competition is fierce, the stakes sky-high. As the years go by, the battle seems to get dirtier and dirtier, the tactics and techniques lower and lower. There is an all-out war going on to get your dollars out of your pocket and into someone else's bank account!

In his book entitled *The Permissible Lie*, Sam Baker, who worked in the advertising industry for thirty years before choosing to leave the profession, exposes the deceptive advertising produced by the inner circles of some of the nation's largest ad agencies. He says, "To increase sales, almost anything goes: misrepresentation, deception, and lies. The goal is to produce the hardest-selling campaign without perpetrating recognizable fraud."

To illustrate, he tells a story of a meeting of advertisers for a specific company. One of the corporate leaders said, "Our top canned goods item is slipping. We need some new excitement in the advertising. We are going to redesign the label to give it a new look, so come up with a new, improved campaign. Lots of big promises. Show us layouts in a week so we can move fast." Someone asked, "Will there be anything new or improved inside the can?" The client blared, "What the %#?+@ kind of question is that? I would have told you if we had made any changes other than the label. The label will be redesigned and the product will look new and improved. Whose side are you on, anyhow?" The questioner wasn't on any side for very long. He was fired from the agency.

4 Take time as a group to evaluate the message and the level of honesty in this advertisement.

5 What are some of the common deceptions in advertisements?

All natural (is it good for you
46% less fat than what

How can you learn to become sensitive to these lies and resist their magnetic appeal?

Be sheptical. Ask other
people. & listen.

Read Snapshot " 'I Want It All, and I Want It Now' "

"I WANT IT ALL, AND I WANT IT NOW"

The second major threat to financial freedom is the availability of easy credit. I saw a bumper sticker once that said "I want it all, and I want it now." Doesn't that say it all? This little saying summarizes the worldview of so many people today. Never before has there been a society more committed to a "Live for the day" philosophy. Yesterday is gone, tomorrow may never come. I want it all, and I want it now.

We want fast food, fast service, mail-order diplomas, a comfortable standard of living, quicker computers, and high-speed everything. Almost every product you can think of is promoted with the phrase, "easy monthly payments." The question is, easy for whom?

In the past people actually had to qualify for credit cards. Now anyone can get a steady stream of them in the mail. Companies are begging people to use their credit cards. These plastic man-eaters can devour you before you realize they are coming. I once talked with a gentleman who said, "I am in deep financial trouble. Can you meet with me?" He was an old friend. I sat down with him and after hearing about his financial trouble I had to respond honestly, "You are in serious trouble. I don't know what you are going to do." He had all his credit cards up to the max. He couldn't make his minimum monthly payments. We talked about some ideas for reducing debt, but then he called me a couple weeks later and said, "I solved the problem." "You solved the problem already?" He said, "Yeah, Visa just sent me another card and now I am borrowing on that to make my minimum monthly payments to my other cards." He thought he was smart, but in reality he was sinking in a sea of debt.

---

6 What are some of the dangers of the credit game?

How have you experienced the seductive lure of easy credit?

7 What are some practical strategies for getting out of credit trouble?

Cut up cards. Don't buy what you can't afford now.

If you struggle in this area, how can your group members keep you accountable to avoid further credit trouble?

Read Snapshot "When Spending Spins Out of Control"

WHEN SPENDING SPINS OUT OF CONTROL

We all need to watch out for the lure of deceitful advertising and the black hole of easy credit. If we avoid these two pitfalls, we will be so much better off. A third area in which people stumble is in undisciplined budgeting practices. Most people groan when they hear the word "budgeting." Mentioning budgeting is about as popular as encouraging people to diet!

But let's try to look at budgeting from another perspective. What if someone disconnected your fuel gauge without telling you? Within a very short time most people would have it fixed. Why? Because you want to know how much gas you still have in your tank. You don't want to be driving around and all of a sudden run out of fuel! A fuel gauge is a lot like a budget; it helps you know how much is coming in and how much is going out. A budget tells you if you are going to run out or if you have plenty.

What do many of us do? We operate our personal finances just like a person who drives a car without a fuel gauge. We go from day to day with no sense of how much we have spent, and then, in the middle of the month, we say, "Oops. I am out of money. I guess now I have to borrow."

8 Finish *one* of the statements below:

- I have never lived with a budget, but I wish I knew how to . . .

- I have budgeted in the past, but can't seem to stay on my budget. I wish someone could explain . . .

- I live with a clear budget and have learned . . .

THE FREEDOM OF BUDGETING

Believe me, a budget is one of the best friends a person can have. You should set a new budget every year. First, assess what your income will be. Next, decide what portion will go to God's work. The biblical model is to give the first ten percent to God, but some will be led to give more than ten percent because they have experienced provision well beyond what they need. Third, determine how much is going to go into savings. Even when you don't have a large income, the discipline and habit of saving is critical.

Next, it is important to lay out your regular monthly expenses. Be specific and realistic about all your regular bills. Go right down the list, set an amount of money for each, and then say, "That's it. That is our budget for this year." Commit yourself to hold to those amounts. This approach will help lead you to financial freedom. Whether you make $20,000 or $200,000, you can be freer than you are today if you watch out for deceitful advertising and easy credit, and commit yourself to a budget.

Take time in the coming week to lay out a basic budget. First, specify what you will give to God. Next, decide what you will put into savings on a weekly or monthly basis. Third, make a detailed list of each area of monthly spending and how much you will allow yourself to spend. Finally, struggle to stay within this budget. It may seem confining, but it is truly freeing.

READY FOR TRUE RICHES?

Over the years I have been deeply challenged by Luke 16:10–12. It says:

> Whoever can be trusted with very little can also be trusted with much, and whoever is dishonest with very little will also be dishonest with much. So if you have not been trustworthy in handling worldly wealth, who will trust you with true riches? And if you have not been trustworthy with someone else's property, who will give you property of your own?

You see, financial freedom is *not* the final goal. You should not leave this small group study saying, "The goal in life is to be financially free." Attaining financial freedom should just serve to liberate you to pursue the more important endeavors of life. We are called to love the Lord our God with all our heart, soul, mind, and strength, and serve and love our neighbors as ourselves.

Take time in the coming week to pray for God to lead you to financial freedom. Pray for your motivation to be right. Pray that discovering this new freedom will release you to love God more and to love and serve others.

GETTING A GRIP ON YOUR SPIRITUAL LIFE

REFLECTIONS FROM SESSION 4

1. If you have begun budgeting for the first time, describe one way this new practice is impacting your life.
2. If you have been reflecting on the ultimate goals of financial freedom, how has this been leading you toward a deeper love for God and others?

THE BIG PICTURE

Every church has people who go to church out of habit. They have been churchgoing people all their lives, and it is almost as automatic as breathing. Every Sunday they go to a church service that feels right to them—one that is comfortable, painless, beautiful, entertaining, or inspirational. They don't really tune in to what is happening. They don't apply what they hear. But they are in church like clockwork.

There are also those who attend church and perform their "religious duties" to silence a spouse, child, or parent. In other words, the conflict is so great when they don't go, they figure the best way to avoid the weekly battle is to acquiesce. These people endure church simply to keep peace in the family. They can't wait until it is over.

Some people attend worship services because they are paying some form of penance. They keep track of their unethical decisions, harsh words, dishonest transactions, immoral acts,

43

and other sins, and by the end of the week they say, "I had better go to church. I have to pay for what I have done this week." For these people, church is a punishment. After enduring an hour of church, they leave with a clean slate, all ready to get muddied up again the next week.

Others go to church to meet people. They find a popular singles' ministry, a hot youth group, or a good social setting and jump right in. Some come to build relationships for business purposes. They see church as another place to network and develop their clientele base. Used right, church can be one of their most profitable hours of the week. They might even be able to write off their offering as a business expense!

Still others attend church because they are just flat-out bored. Who wants to go to work on a Sunday morning, after all? And television programs on Sunday morning aren't all that hot. Getting out for church is just a way to kill a few hours on a slow morning.

Certainly, many people attend church because they are hoping that something during the service—the Scripture reading, the music ministry, the singing, the drama, or some part of the sermon—will trigger something new in their heart. They hunger for a spiritual discovery that will help them understand more about God. They want to learn how they can love Him more, how to feel inspired to live for Him, or how to change the course of some behavior. They want to go the next step in their Christian life.

A WIDE ANGLE VIEW

1 How would you describe your attitude and motivation when you first started attending church?

It had been a while. I was hungry for spiritual nourishment the world had too & didn't want to.

What moves you to attend church today?

The message & the drama of my bible study. I enjoy it.

A BIBLICAL PORTRAIT

Read Hebrews 4:14–16; 10:19–25

2 Some followers of Christ struggle with feeling that God is angry with them and does not want them entering His presence. How do these passages destroy that false mind-set?

That Through Jesus we can go to God when we need to. We don't have to wait till were better Christians

3 What has God done so that we can approach His throne any time, any place, with boldness and confidence?

By the blood of Jesus. He is the new way. (Through the curtain)

Why would God go to such lengths just to be in relationship with us?

God is a just God & can't have sin unpunished & so he sent Jesus to pay for our sins - He sees us through Jesus colored Glasses

Read Snapshot "The Militaristic Approach"

THE MILITARISTIC APPROACH

One approach to improving your companionship, relationship, and dialogue with God is what I will call the "militaristic" approach. You may already know what I am talking about. Most of us have heard Christian leaders say, "If you are ever going to improve your relationship with God, you need to get up every morning at 6 A.M. and spend at least thirty minutes with God—fifteen minutes reading the Bible and fifteen minutes in prayer. If you do this on a daily basis, you are all set. Get up early, do the devotional thing, and you have covered your spiritual bases for the day!"

4 What are some advantages to this approach to your relationship with Christ? *Start day off right, Help to keep Gods word in your life, Gives God a chance to talk to you. Helps you to become closer to him.*

What are some disadvantages? *Takes time + discipline*

Psalm ALL 19: 12-14

would become mundane.

5 Respond to *one* of these statements:

- If a follower of Christ does not spend fifteen to thirty minutes in the Word every day, they just don't measure up to God's standard.
- If I don't spend the first fifteen minutes of my day on my knees in prayer, I just can't go on. This is the only way to start a day! By the way . . . what do *you* do first thing in the morning?

JESSIE

- The key to a real and deep Christian faith is having a daily, consistent, and in-depth devotional time of Bible study and prayer. There is no other way to spiritual growth.
- I like to get my devotional time over first thing in the morning so I can move on with my day.

This will be new for me but I do read the bible & pray at night before bed. I feel any time at all would be helpful. This ⊘ paragraph is still more religious than I believe.

Read Snapshot "The Libertarian Approach"

THE LIBERTARIAN APPROACH

On the opposite extreme of the devotional spectrum you find what I will call the "libertarian" approach to building a relationship with God. Libertarians are those people who seek spiritual growth when it feels right. They attend church when they happen to wake up on time. They read their Bible when they feel like it. They pray when there is an urgent and pressing need. They like to say things like, "I don't usually go to church. I get more out of sitting alone in a forest preserve for an hour." Any set form, discipline, schedule, or established time pattern seems to offend their free-flowing spirit. They say, "I will build my relationship with God as the Spirit moves me and when the Spirit moves me."

6

What are some of the pitfalls of this approach to growing as a follower of Christ? *Never grow. God is last. No relationship there.*

What are some signs that a person is approaching their faith with a libertarian mind-set? *Backlash, ??? sliding.*

7

Where do you see this mind-set in *one* of these areas:

- In the church at large
- In your local church
- In your own life

I used to be that way.
Spirituality not that important

Read Snapshot "The Creative-Relational Approach"

THE CREATIVE-RELATIONAL APPROACH

God doesn't want a half-hour of your time; He wants to be a part of every single moment of every single day. He wants you to be aware of His presence as you wake up, as you go through your day, and as you put your head on the pillow at night. He wants to be in the center of your life in the family room, the boardroom, the classroom, and the laundry room. He wants your devotional life to permeate the totality of your life. And He wants it to be real, not mechanical.

Think about it in terms of a human relationship. Imagine if you took a week off from work and spent each day with this person. You show up at his house at seven o'clock in the morning and have breakfast with his family. You ride in his car to work, watch him fight his way through traffic and find a parking place, sit in his office, listen to his conversations, meet his coworkers, and watch him handle all his daily tasks. You ride home with him at night, share dinner, and then go for a run in the evening. Imagine what could happen to a relationship if you creatively spent each day together!

Now imagine what could happen in your relationship with God if you invited Him to be part of every aspect of your life. Of course Bible study is important. Do it regularly and God will teach you great things. Of course prayer is essential, but don't limit your conversation with God to fifteen minutes in the morning and a few quick prayers before meals. Instead, talk with Him all day long. Let praise pour out of your mouth in the car as you drive, in the shower, around your house. Read Christian books and listen to Christian music. Connect with other followers of Christ on a regular basis to encourage, sharpen, and inspire each other. Let your relationship with God be creative, dynamic, and fill every aspect of your life.

8

How have you experienced an open relationship and communication with God through the course of your daily activities?

Talk to him & pray when at work
Talk about him w/ co workers.

Let go & pray for answers

9

What tends to keep you from experiencing this creative and dynamic interaction with God in *one* of these spheres of life:

- In the workplace
- In your home
- In church settings
- In your recreational pursuits
- In any other areas of your life

Trying to do it ourselves + not listening

RECEIVING FROM GOD

One essential ingredient in the "creative-relational" approach to growth is spending time reading and learning from the Bible. Start with a small New Testament book, like James, Philippians, or Colossians. Then go to a Christian bookstore and buy a little commentary. A commentary is a tool that helps you understand the difficult parts of what you are reading. Read a section of verses, read what the commentary has to say about those verses, and pray about how you can apply the passage to your life. You may want to tell a friend what you have learned and how you plan to live out this truth. Keep reading, section by section, until you finish the whole book.

Then, before you dive headlong into another book of the Bible, take a few days off. Put the Bible on the shelf, find a couple of highly recommended Christian books, and spend a few days reading them. Or ask your pastor to recommend a good book for where you are in your spiritual growth curve.

You can also mix in some Bible memorization. Pick a passage that really impacts you and commit it to memory. This might be your time of focus on God's Word for a few days. You might even want to get some sermons on tape and listen to them with your Bible open in front of you.

Think about the coming two weeks and lay out a plan for at least three different ways to learn from Scripture. Ask a friend to pray for you and keep you accountable as you learn to get creative in your relationship with God.

In the coming two weeks I will grow in God's Word through:

_____

_____

_____

_____

A PLACE FOR PRAYER

Have you ever tried to pray for fifteen minutes each morning and found your mind wandering? People tell you to pray, so you sit down with your list of names and needs and begin cranking through them. After a few days, this can become dry and routine. But the Bible never says that longer prayers are better prayers. The Bible simply calls us to pour out our hearts to our heavenly Father. We are not called to lift up mindless and repetitious prayers and praises. Instead, just talk openly with God. Improve your dialogue with him.

As you talk you will discover that there are several different kinds of prayers. *Closet prayers* are those where you go away to a quiet place and spend focused time in prayer for needs and burdens you carry as well as lifting up your praises. *Catch prayers* happen throughout the day where you find yourself saying, "Lord, help me, give me wisdom, help that person in need, watch over my children, thanks for Your presence," and whatever else comes to heart.

There are also *written prayers.* Put a blank piece of paper in front of you and write "Yesterday" on the top, "Today" in the middle, and "Tomorrow" near the bottom. Once you have that, begin pouring out your heart to God through writing. Or maybe you'll find yourself driving along, lifting your voice in a praise chorus or hymn. Let these words become your prayer. The key is to communicate with God. He cares about you and wants to hear your joys and sorrows.

In your prayer life this week, try to note the different ways you communicate with God. Write down a few of your observations in the space below:

Where were you when you prayed?

- _____
- _____
- _____
- _____

What moved you to pray?

- _____
- _____
- _____
- _____

What kind of prayers did you lift to God? If you don't have an official name for a specific kind of prayer, make one up:

- _____
- _____
- _____
- _____

GETTING A GRIP ON YOUR RELATIONSHIPS

REFLECTIONS FROM SESSION 5

1. If you have been experiencing creativity in your study of the Bible, how has this breathed vitality into your spiritual life?

2. If you have been taking note of your prayer life over the past week, tell your group what you have discovered. What kinds of prayer have you been moved to lift up to God?

THE BIG PICTURE

As you begin this session, you will be taking a fill-in-the-blank quiz. There are no right or wrong answers; you will not be graded. All you need to do is write in the name of a person (or persons) after each scenario. Some of these scenarios might not apply to where you are in life right now. Still, try to imagine if you were in this circumstance, whose name would come to mind.

1. After missing your original connecting flight, you have finally arrived at the airport at midnight. Who would you call to come pick you up and take you home?

   Name: _____

2. You have been working like crazy to get a shot at an exciting promotion at work. The promotion means

increased responsibility and opportunities, and much more pay. You really don't think you are going to get it, but one day your supervisor comes in and says, "The position is yours." Apart from a spouse or an immediate family member, who would you call to tell the good news and invite to share your joy?

Name: _____

3. You and your spouse have been trying to conceive a child for more than three years. Finally you get the test back. You are going to have a baby! Who do you call first to tell the good news?

Name: _____

4. Things have not been going well at home. Tensions are high both at work and in your marriage. Your spiritual life is as dry as the Sahara Desert. You need to talk with somebody; to confide in someone who cares and who will keep things confidential. Who could you call who will be straight with you and who will be able to provide you with some decent counsel?

Name: _____

5. You are bored stiff. You want to call someone to go out to a show or to go out to dinner with. Who do you call?

Name: _____

6. You have just won a two-week, all expenses paid Hawaii vacation. If you are a married couple you get to invite another married couple to come with you. If you are single, you get to invite a friend. Who would you invite?

Name: _____

A WIDE ANGLE VIEW

1 Identify one person you named on your quiz and tell why you chose to call that person.

How would your life be changed if you were no longer in relationship with this person?

A BIBLICAL PORTRAIT

Read Genesis 2:15–23; Psalm 133:1

2 What does Genesis 2:15–23 tell you about our need for human relationships?

3 What are some outward indications that people are experiencing unity in a relationship?

What are some of the indications that they are experiencing disunity?

Read Snapshot "Putting an End to Aloneness"

PUTTING AN END TO ALONENESS

One reason for pursuing strong, meaningful relationships is to put an end to aloneness. In Genesis 2:18 God said it is not good for man to be alone. Another way of saying this is that human beings were created for community. We are not living up to our God-given potential as human beings if we try to lead Lone Ranger lives. God, in His grace, provided a way to end our aloneness. He designed us to lead deep, authentic relationships—in community—with other people. We were intended to communicate, to give and take, to love and be loved, to serve and be served.

4 Describe a time you have experienced loneliness.

How have meaningful relationships helped you through a lonely time?

Read Snapshot "Meaningful Relationships Multiply Our Joy"

MEANINGFUL RELATIONSHIPS MULTIPLY OUR JOY

A second reason for pursuing strong interpersonal relationships is that developing relationships allows us to multiply our joys. In the gospel of Luke, chapter 15, we find stories about a lost sheep, a lost coin, and a lost son who wanders away from home. In each of these cases, when that which is lost is found, there is great rejoicing! When the lost treasure is finally discovered, it's time to call friends together to come and celebrate. "That which was lost is now found. Let's party!"

It is almost impossible to experience joy and not share it. What happens when a young woman gets engaged? She can't contain the joy she feels. She wants to share that joy with other people. Similarly, we feel like we are going to explode if we don't let others know the joys we may be experiencing.

5 What is one joy you are experiencing in your life right now?

Read Snapshot "Meaningful Relationships Divide Our Sorrows"

6 Describe a time others came alongside you and helped carry a burden you were facing.

What is one load you are carrying right now that your small group members could help carry?

Read Snapshot "Meaningful Relationships Afford Us Counsel"

MEANINGFUL RELATIONSHIPS AFFORD US COUNSEL

A fourth reason for pursuing strong relationships is that they offer us counsel and perspective. Proverbs 11:14 says, "For lack of guidance a nation falls, but many advisers make victory sure." Even the wisest of people needs counsel and wisdom from others. I often wonder how many bumps, bruises, heartaches, and sorrows could be avoided if we would only learn to seek counsel before we make decisions.

Presidents, rulers, prime ministers, and world leaders surround themselves with counselors because they know their decisions have grave consequences. They are committed to getting perspective from peers they respect. The decisions we make may not have implications on the direction of nations, but they are still very important. We need to learn the importance of seeking the counsel of others when making major life decisions, and even when making decisions that don't seem so critical! Seeking counsel almost always helps and is rarely regretted.

7 Tell your group members about a life situation you are facing right now in *one* of the areas listed below. Invite them to offer counsel and perspective.

- In the workplace
- In a family relationship
- In a friendship
- In a ministry situation
- In your neighborhood
- In some other area of life

Read Snapshot "Meaningful Relationships Create a Place for Accountability"

MEANINGFUL RELATIONSHIPS CREATE A PLACE FOR ACCOUNTABILITY

A fifth reason for developing strong relationships is to create a place for intentional accountability. I had spoken to a group of Christian leaders about the importance of community and relationships. After I finished speaking, one of the men in attendance broke into the conversation and said, "I want to affirm that what we have just heard about community and relationships is God's Word." But then he went on to say, "But I want to announce to all of you that I have enough truth about this topic. What I need now is a few brothers to help me apply these truths for the rest of my life." He declared, "I don't have to *learn* more in this area, I need to *conform* more. I need people to hold me accountable and help me practice the truth I just heard."

What a refreshing and honest response! We need to commit ourselves to one another and say, "Hold me to the truth." We must invite others into our lives and say, "Cheer me on. Encourage me. Challenge me. Redirect me. Correct me. Do whatever you have to do because I want to live out God's truth . . . not just know it." This rare and powerful practice is called accountability, and it should be a central part of our relationships.

8
Describe someone who keeps you accountable
and how this relationship has helped you grow as
a follower of Christ.

9
What is one area in which your small group members
can pray for you, encourage you, and keep you
accountable?

PUTTING YOURSELF IN THE PICTURE

ENDING LONELINESS

In this lesson we discussed that relationships help put an end
to our loneliness. Who is one person in your life that you sus-
pect may be facing some kind of loneliness today? Maybe he
or she has lost a loved one, gone through a time of illness, or is
simply dealing with some tough times in life. Give that person a call and set a date to get together. Plan to take a walk,
have a meal together, or visit for an evening. Be intentional
about helping put an end to the loneliness of others.

BURDEN ASSESSMENT

Take a blank sheet of paper and write down three burdens
you are carrying right now. They can be emotional, relational,
professional, physical . . . any kind of burden. After you have

written down these burdens, make a list of the people you have asked to help you bear them. If you have never asked anyone to help you bear a burden, think of some people in your life who could help you with these burdens. Commit yourself to contacting these people within twenty-four hours. Tell them about what you are facing and ask them for their prayers and support. You will be amazed at how many people are excited and willing to help you bear your burdens. In some cases, they have been waiting for you to ask!

LEADER'S NOTES

Leading a Bible discussion—especially for the first time—can make you feel both nervous and excited. If you are nervous, realize that you are in good company. Many biblical leaders, such as Moses, Joshua, and the apostle Paul, felt nervous and inadequate to lead others (see, for example, 1 Cor. 2:3). Yet God's grace was sufficient for them, just as it will be for you.

Some excitement is also natural. Your leadership is a gift to the others in the group. Keep in mind, however, that other group members also share responsibility for the group. Your role is simply to stimulate discussion by asking questions and encouraging people to respond. The suggestions listed below can help you to be an effective leader.

PREPARING TO LEAD

1. Ask God to help you understand and apply the passage to your own life. Unless that happens, you will not be prepared to lead others.
2. Carefully work through each question in the study guide. Meditate and reflect on the passage as you formulate your answers.
3. Familiarize yourself with the Leader's Notes for each session. These will help you understand the purpose of the session and will provide valuable information about the questions in the session. The Leader's Notes are not intended to be read to the group. These notes are primarily for your use as a group leader and for your preparation. However, when you find a section that relates well to your group, you may want to read a brief portion or encourage them to read this section at another time.
4. Pray for the various members of the group. Ask God to use these sessions to make you better disciples of Jesus Christ.
5. Before the first session, make sure each person has a study guide. Encourage them to prepare beforehand for each session.

LEADING THE SESSION

1. Begin the session on time. If people realize that the session begins on schedule, they will work harder to arrive on time.

2. At the beginning of your first time together, explain that these sessions are designed to be discussions, not lectures. Encourage everyone to participate, but realize some may be hesitant to speak during the first few sessions.

3. Don't be afraid of silence. People in the group may need time to think before responding.

4. Avoid answering your own questions. If necessary, rephrase a question until it is clearly understood. Even an eager group will quickly become passive and silent if they think the leader will do most of the talking.

5. Encourage more than one answer to each question. Ask, "What do the rest of you think?" or "Anyone else?" until several people have had a chance to respond.

6. Try to be affirming whenever possible. Let people know you appreciate their insights into the passage.

7. Never reject an answer. If it is clearly wrong, ask, "Which verse led you to that conclusion?" Or let the group handle the problem by asking them what they think about the question.

8. Avoid going off on tangents. If people wander off course, gently bring them back to the passage being considered.

9. Conclude your time together with conversational prayer. Ask God to help you apply those things that you learned in the session.

10. End on time. This will be easier if you control the pace of the discussion by not spending too much time on some questions or too little on others.

We encourage all small group leaders to use *Leading Life-Changing Small Groups* (Zondervan) by Bill Donahue and the Willow Creek Small Group Team while leading their group. Developed and used by Willow Creek Community Church, this guide is an excellent resource for training and equipping followers of Christ to effectively lead small groups. It includes valuable information on how to utilize fun and creative relationship-building exercises for your group; how to plan your meeting; how to share the leadership load by identifying, developing, and working with an "apprentice leader"; and how to find creative ways to do group prayer. In addition, the book includes material and tips on handling potential conflicts and difficult personalities, forming group covenants, inviting new members, improving listening skills, studying the Bible, and much more. Using *Leading Life-Changing Small Groups* will help you create a group that members love to be a part of.

Now let's discuss the different elements of this small group study guide and how to use them for the session portion of your group meeting.

THE BIG PICTURE

Each session will begin with a short story or overview of the lesson theme. This is called "The Big Picture" because it introduces the central theme of the session. You will need to read this section as a group or have group members read it on their own before discussion begins. Here are three ways you can approach this section of the small group session:

- As the group leader, read this section out loud for the whole group and then move into the questions in the next section, "A Wide Angle View." (You might read the first week, but then use the other two options below to encourage group involvement.)

- Ask a group member to volunteer to read this section for the group. This allows another group member to participate. It is best to ask someone in advance to give them time to read over the section before reading it to the group. It is also good to ask someone to volunteer, and not to assign this task. Some people do not feel comfortable reading in front of a group. After a group member has read this section out loud, move into the discussion questions.

- Allow time at the beginning of the session for each person to read this section silently. If you do this, be sure to allow enough time for everyone to finish reading so they can think about what they've read and be ready for meaningful discussion.

A WIDE ANGLE VIEW

This section includes one or more questions that move the group into a general discussion of the session topic. These questions are designed to help group members begin discussing the topic in an open and honest manner. Once the topic of the lesson has been established, move on to the Bible passage for the session.

A BIBLICAL PORTRAIT

This portion of the session includes a Scripture reading and one or more questions that help group members see how the theme of the session is rooted and based in biblical teaching. The Scripture reading can be handled just like "The Big Picture" section: You can read it for the group, have a group member read it, or allow time for silent reading. Make sure everyone has a Bible or that you have Bibles available for those who need them. Once you have read the passage, ask the question(s) in this section so that group members can dig into the truth of the Bible.

SHARPENING THE FOCUS

The majority of the discussion questions for the session are in this section. These questions are practical and help group members apply biblical teaching to their daily lives.

SNAPSHOTS

The "Snapshots" in each session help prepare group members for discussion. These anecdotes give additional insight to the topic being discussed. Each "Snapshot" should be read at a designated point in the session. This is clearly marked in the session as well as in the Leader's Notes. Again, follow the same format as you do with "The Big Picture" section and the "Biblical Portrait" section: Either you read the anecdote, have a group member volunteer to read, or provide time for silent reading. However you approach this section, you will find these anecdotes very helpful in triggering lively dialogue and moving discussion in a meaningful direction.

PUTTING YOURSELF IN THE PICTURE

Here's where you roll up your sleeves and put the truth into action. This portion is very practical and action-oriented. At the end of each session there will be suggestions for one or two ways group members can put what they've just learned into practice. Review the action goals at the end of each session and challenge group members to work on one or more of them in the coming week.

You will find follow-up questions for the "Putting Yourself in the Picture" section at the beginning of the next week's session. Starting with the second week, there will be time set aside at the beginning of the session to look back and talk about how you have tried to apply God's Word in your life since your last time together.

PRAYER

You will want to open and close your small group with a time of prayer. Occasionally, there will be specific direction within a session for how you can do this. Most of the time, however, you will need to decide the best place to stop and pray. You may want to pray or have a group member volunteer to begin the lesson with a prayer. Or you might want to read "The Big Picture" and discuss the "Wide Angle View" questions before opening in prayer. In some cases, it might be best to open in prayer after you have read the Bible passage. You need to decide where you feel an opening prayer best fits for your group.

When opening in prayer, think in terms of the session theme and pray for group members (including yourself) to be responsive to the truth of Scripture and the working of the Holy Spirit. If you have seekers in your group (people investigating Christianity but not yet believers), be sensitive to your expectations for group prayer. Seekers may not yet be ready to take part in group prayer.

Be sure to close your group with a time of prayer as well. One option is for you to pray for the entire group. Or you might allow time for group members to offer audible prayers that others can agree with in their hearts. Another approach would be to allow a time of silence for one-on-one prayers with God and then to close this time with a simple "Amen."

GETTING A GRIP ON YOUR LIFE

Genesis 1:1–27

INTRODUCTION

No one likes being out of control. We all have a built-in desire and need for order in our lives. All of us desire to have a grip on our lives. The question is, how?

Most of us have tried the regular list of New Year's resolutions and have thrown in the towel before the end of January. We have been moved, motivated, and manipulated to make the big commitments, only to watch our lives continue spinning out of control.

Yet, we keep trying. We go on one more diet and commit to a new exercise program. We buy a new planner and declare that this year we will master our schedule rather than have our schedule master us. We get out our Bible, buy a blank journal, and say, "This is the year I'm going to get face-to-face with God." We mean business! We are serious! But we still struggle.

This series of studies will help you walk through some critical areas of life that we all want to have under control. But the first and essential step is to take an honest and rigorous look at your life. If you can't be honest with yourself and the members of your small group, it will be tough to get a grip on these areas. Open your heart to what God wants to do, be painfully honest, and anticipate great things in the weeks to come. God wants to see you get a grip on your life even more than you do!

THE BIG PICTURE

Take time to read this introduction with the group. There are suggestions for how this can be done in the beginning of the leader's section.

A WIDE ANGLE VIEW

Question One We all have stories to tell. Some will be humorous and others very serious. Inviting group members to tell their stories will be a great way to learn some of their personal history as well as hear about how they have responded to times when they were out of control.

A Biblical Portrait

Read Genesis 1:1–27

Question Two Genesis teaches that God created the beauty of this world out of shapeless, chaotic nothingness. Not only did He bring order to chaos, the order He established is extraordinary. Just look at the world around you: the colors, the animal life, the ecosystems, the planets in orbit—all of this was put in place by the hand of a powerful and orderly Creator.

Even the succession of days in Genesis and the progression of what God made shows purpose and order. The very nature and character of God is seen in creation. He made it all and grips it firmly in His hand. We are not set adrift in a sea of space, but are safely under the control of a loving and powerful Creator.

Question Three I suppose part of the reason we feel such discomfort when something in our own lives is out of control is because we have been made in the image of an orderly Creator. Just look at creation, the sequence of the seasons, the regularity of the sunrise, the symmetry of the human body, and the movement of the celestial bodies. There is no denying that God is an orderly Creator.

We are made in the image of an orderly Creator, and have been called to live well-ordered lives. God has given us guidelines and laws to help order our lives. He never intended for us to live in chaos. He knew we could never enjoy life if we were spinning out of control.

He didn't ordain straightjacket living and legalistically regimented lives. But He does want us to live with some form of balance and order. If God's character is one of order, and we have been made in His image, then we will find the greatest level of fulfillment in life when we reflect the character of an orderly Creator.

Sharpening the Focus

Read Snapshot "An Honest Look at Your Life" before Question 4

Question Four Three pie graphs are given as examples. Each one gives a window into what a person's life might look like.

Take time as a group to unpack some of the implications of each life represented.

Question Five Now we are moving from the abstract to the concrete. Let's stop talking about some hypothetical person on a pie graph and take a good look into a mirror at ourselves. This is a tender topic. Many people spend a great deal of time and energy to be sure no one ever sees the picture they are about to draw (including themselves).

As you enter this portion of the study, do so prayerfully and with great sensitivity. For some, this kind of self-examination and self-disclosure may come easily. For others, there may be resistance and fear. You may want to pause as a group for a brief time of prayer. Ask for God to grant courage to each group member as they reflect on their life.

Questions Six & Seven Begin with the positive. Celebrate the areas where group members are experiencing control. Rejoice that they have a grip on these areas of life. Next, reflect on those areas where there is a desire to get a grip. Don't talk about these as areas of failure, but lift them up as areas where there is a deep desire to see the particular area come under control.

**Read Snapshot "It's Time to Get a Grip"
before Question 8**

Questions Eight & Nine Now we are going to get very specific. There will be five primary areas of focus in the rest of this study. Take time for personal reflection on each area. Give a few minutes for group members to quietly pray, think about, and mark where they see themselves in each of the five areas. When you pull back together, the focus will not be an all-out disclosure of every area; simply invite group members to communicate one area in which they desire prayer from the other group members. This could form a great prayer list for the coming weeks as well as direction for prayer as you close your group.

Also encourage group members to celebrate one area where there is strength. One person's story of having a grip in a particular area might just give another group member the inspiration they need to believe God can help them gain control of this area in their life.

PUTTING YOURSELF IN THE PICTURE

Tell group members that you will be providing time at the beginning of the next meeting for them to discuss how they have put their faith into action. Let them tell their stories; however, don't limit their interaction to the two options provided. They may have put themselves into the picture in some other way as a result of your study. Allow for honest and open communication.

Also, be clear that there will not be any kind of a "test" or forced reporting. All you are going to do is allow time for people to volunteer to talk about how they have applied what they learned in your last study. Some group members will feel pressured if they think you are going to make everyone provide a "report." You don't want anyone to skip the next group because they are afraid of having to say they did not follow up on what they learned from the prior session. The key is to provide a place for honest communication without creating pressure and fear of being embarrassed.

Every session from this point on will open with a look back at the "Putting Yourself in the Picture" section of the previous session.

GETTING A GRIP ON YOUR SCHEDULE

Ecclesiastes 3:1–13; Ephesians 5:15–20

INTRODUCTION

Trying to tame a schedule in our insanely busy world may seem impossible. It seems the pressure to move faster, produce more, and accomplish greater things never lets up. On the freeway of life, if you don't keep up the pace, you get run over!

In the midst of our pathologically fast-paced society, God calls us to get a grip on our schedule. We are called to move from imbalance to a place where God has control of every aspect of our lives. This is not only possible, it is what God expects of His followers.

THE BIG PICTURE

Take time to read this introduction with the group. There are suggestions for how this can be done in the beginning of the leader's section.

A WIDE ANGLE VIEW

Question One Contelmo writes his article with tongue in cheek. We will never build a relationship with God on ten minutes a day. It can't be done. We would like to think we can build a relationship with God in the same way we pick up a burger in the drive-thru lane at McDonald's. But a deep relationship with God requires energy, concentration, devotion, regular church attendance, Bible study, small groups, prayer, confession, and a lifetime of growth. There is no such thing as microwave Christianity.

A BIBLICAL PORTRAIT

Read Ecclesiastes 3:1–13; Ephesians 5:15–20

Question Two There is a time for everything, says Ecclesiastes. This means we are given the awesome task of discerning and deciding what needs to be done today. Every day we face countless options; we simply can't do everything. Part of growing as a follower of Christ is knowing what we need to do today, what can wait until tomorrow, and what does not need to be done at all!

Think of the words of Jesus in Matthew 6:34: "Therefore do not worry about tomorrow, for tomorrow will worry about itself. Each day has enough trouble of its own." With all the things we could do, we need to learn to ask the question, "What does God want me to do today?" God will never call us to do more than we can handle. When we get overextended and burned-out, that is our own doing.

Question Three This passage gives some general insights on how to use and not use our time. Encourage group members to draw these insights from the text. Finish your reflection on this biblical text by inviting group members to summarize the meaning of Paul's teaching in their own words. You may want to give a minute or two for group members to reflect on this and maybe even have them write down a clear sentence putting this message in their own words.

SHARPENING THE FOCUS

Read Snapshot "A Life Out of Balance" before Question 4

Questions Four & Five You may want to encourage group members to look back at the pie graph they drew in session one, question five. This may help prime the pump for discussion. All of us have areas to which we are devoting too much time and other areas that require greater focus and energy. Honest discussion about this will free each person to face areas in which they need to grow.

One area that will probably come up for many people is an overemphasis on work. Some are *addicted* to work, while others simply allocate large segments of their pie to work. When a large portion of our pie is taken up with vocational pursuits, the rest of the dimensions get crowded out and neglected. When this happens, you don't have time or energy to be the type of spouse, parent, or friend you need to be.

A Cornell University professor did a study to determine the average amount of time fathers spend with their small children on a daily basis. The professor actually put microphones on fathers and little children and recorded the direct interaction between them. They gathered the data, analyzed the results, and announced that the average amount of time the middle-class father spends with his small child is 37.7 seconds *per day*. Put that data on one side of the spectrum and then consider this: The average amount of time the middle-class child spends watching television per week in the preschool years is 54 hours. The next question is obvious: Who is raising that child? Who is influencing that little life? If our schedule is out of balance, the damage could be worse than we imagine.

Read Snapshot "A Life in Balance" before Question 6

Questions Six & Seven The picture of a life in balance has the illusion of being the best of all possible scenarios. Isn't balance the best thing? Well, if you look closely, you will see that, although there are some advantages, the place of faith is only one segment of the pie. This approach compartmentalizes faith as one part of life, removed from the rest. The problem with this picture of "balance" is that it is a facade. Keeping Christ in a box, in a compartment, in one little section of life will never work for the person who wants to become a fully devoted follower of Christ. As you will see in "A Life Beyond Balance," Christ should be in the center of every area of life, not just another aspect of life.

Read Snapshot "A Life Beyond Balance" before Question 8

Questions Eight & Nine Christ deserves to be at the center of our life. God doesn't seem to mightily use people who are committed to Him casually. Anything less than radical devotion makes a mockery out of what Christ has done for you.

What happens when Christ is at the center of your life? Think about the pie graph with the cross in the center. Imagine that cross being able to spin around like the pointer on a table game. The Bible says that if Christ is at the center of your life, He will be your guide. He will show the way. That means He will point to which area in your life needs to be emphasized at any given time.

It's rather simplistic to think that we are going to be able to keep all pieces of the pie equal for the rest of our lives. Our life ebbs and flows, and there are times when certain parts of our life will demand more attention. Those who work with distinct seasons understand this concept well. For CPAs, bookkeepers, and accountants, January 15 to April 15 means work up to their ears. During those months, things will feel out of balance. If Christ is at the center of your life and the freedom of the Holy Spirit leads you, the cross will point to your vocational life for that season. When that season is over, the Lord will move you over so you can make it up to your family, make it up recreationally, make it up spiritually.

Mothers with small children face this as well. Theirs is a season of radical focus on family. It may feel out of balance, but it is a time when service in the church and even personal pursuits may need to be put on the back burner. In the middle of it all, though, mothers need to be sure Christ is in the center of their life.

Having Christ in the middle of your life is the best way to handle the calendar monster. It is the most effective way to bring discipline to your schedule. He is the only One who can give you the assurance that your emphasis is right at that time in your life. He is alive, living and dynamic. He can move with the ebb and flow of your life. This is called "walking by the Spirit." There is great freedom in Christ. You can enjoy the confidence of knowing that your schedule is under God's control.

PUTTING YOURSELF IN THE PICTURE

Challenge group members to take time in the coming week to use part or all of this application section as an opportunity for continued growth.

GETTING A GRIP ON YOUR BODY

Romans 12:1–2; 1 Corinthians 6:19–20

INTRODUCTION

Historically, Christians have emphasized the importance of the soul. Regretfully, we have emphasized the soul or spirit to the near exclusion of all the clear teaching in Scripture pertaining to the importance of the body. God certainly cares for souls, but He also cares for our bodies. God sees us as total beings, our body, soul, and spirit bound inextricably together. Dichotomization (splitting ourselves into body and soul) should be avoided at all costs. In short, God is concerned about you and all that makes you who you are. Your personality, your emotional makeup, your temperament, your body, your soul, and your spirit all matter to God. This session highlights what has been so grossly ignored in the church, the importance of our bodies.

THE BIG PICTURE

Take time to read this introduction with the group. There are suggestions for how this can be done in the beginning of the leader's section.

A WIDE ANGLE VIEW

Question One We all have stories to tell about victories and struggles on the battlefield of personal health. Start with the positive. Affirm the victories and steps of growth group members have taken. Then, allow group members to tell a few war stories. By putting this on the table up front, it will ease the tension about being honest about our struggles.

A BIBLICAL PORTRAIT

Read Romans 12:1–2; 1 Corinthians 6:19–20

Questions Two & Three God demonstrated His concern for our bodies in that He chose, by the power of His Holy

Spirit, to dwell in human bodies. In the Old Testament we read that God, at one point in time, decided to focus His presence among His people. In order to do that, He called them to build a tabernacle and, later, a temple. In those places God would periodically focus His presence. When He commanded the people to build the tabernacle and the temple, God was very specific about how they should be constructed. He demanded they be built with elaborate materials and decorations. They were ornate, surrounded by precious items, and impeccably maintained. These buildings were held in awe because God, from time to time, focused His presence there.

In the New Testament, the writers unfold a startling truth. God, they announced, had decided He was going to move. He would have a new address. He was not going to focus His presence in buildings anymore. The apostle Paul and others announced that God would take up residency in the bodies of individual believers.

God thinks so much of human bodies that when people become believers He lives inside each of them in the presence of His Holy Spirit. With this in mind, God has issued a comprehensive command concerning how we should treat our bodies. We are His temples and we should offer ourselves as living sacrifices.

SHARPENING THE FOCUS

Read Snapshot "God Cares About Your Body" before Question 4

Question Four God has richly provided for each of us. Take time as a group to openly celebrate what God has done to prove His concern for you through filling your needs.

Question Five What would change this week if God was physically walking with you through every moment? Could you imagine it? The God who loves you, who gave His Son for you, walking with you each step of the way? What would be different in your week? How would your speech change? How would you use your free time? How would you treat your family, friends, neighbors, colleagues at work? What would change?

In reality, God is with you each moment of every day. He sees what you do, hears what you say, even knows the intentions of your heart. Through the Holy Spirit, God is in and with you at all times.

Read Snapshot "What You Put In Your Body" before Question 6

Question Six This is where the proverbial rubber hits the road. If we are putting junk fuel into our bodies, we can expect poor performance. If we put top-grade fuel in the tanks of our lives, we can expect much better performance.

When we put junk in our systems for years and years and then experience physical deterioration and serious medical problems, we have no right to look angrily at heaven and demand an explanation of God. We wonder why He has arbitrarily chosen to afflict a person as righteous and pious as we are. In reality, we have been abusing our bodies for years, filling them with poisons. It is not God's fault at all.

A ten-year study was done on the effects of a high-cholesterol diet. It was no surprise to discover that a high-cholesterol diet increases blood pressure and produces higher rates of heart attack. A leading nutrition expert asks, "Does the U.S. have a health problem?" Look at it this way: Heart disease was unknown in 1900, but it is a major killer today. Most of the food in America today will support life, but it won't sustain health.

Most health problems underlying the leading causes of death in the U.S. could be modified by improvements in the diet. We buy food for taste, convenience, and according to habit, not according to nutritional needs. Processed foods have increased from ten percent of the American diet in 1940 to over sixty percent today. Forty percent of all Americans are overweight.

In addition, increasing numbers of our children are influenced by advertising, and those children are growing up overweight. Breakfast cereals, cookies, candy, gum, snacks, tarts, and frozen waffles make up about two-thirds of the televised food advertising directed at children. These advertisements have subtle ways of leading children to believe that the product is not only delicious and fun to eat, but even good for them. The foods children are allowed to consume during the first years of life usually become their favorites. We need to begin with ourselves, but also teach the next generation to fill their bodies with fuel that will lead to a high-performance life that will honor God.

Read Snapshot "How You Condition Your Body" before Question 7

Question Seven We can all come up with plenty of reasons why it is hard to exercise and establish a pattern of regular physical conditioning. Be honest about these roadblocks to health and also discuss how you can remove them. Invite other group members to encourage you, pray for you, and keep you accountable. You might even find a commitment to walk, run, or exercise together. Partnering up is one great way to create regular accountability in this area of life.

Read Snapshot "How You Use Your Body" before Question 8

Questions Eight & Nine Finish your session by expressing practical goals for growth in getting a grip on your personal health. The goals will vary: running on a regular basis, changing eating habits, quitting smoking, getting more sleep, or some other practical sign of desired growth in this area. Be sure to close the group by praying for those who have committed to a specific growth goal toward getting a grip on their body.

PUTTING YOURSELF IN THE PICTURE

Challenge group members to take some time in the coming week to use part or all of this application section as an opportunity for continued growth.

GETTING A GRIP ON YOUR FINANCES

*1 Timothy 6:6–10;
Proverbs 30:8–9; Hebrews 13:5*

INTRODUCTION

The goal of this session is to instruct and inspire you to get a grip on your money. The money monster is a hard character to pin down—after all, we live in a culture obsessed with earning, saving, and spending it! We have all been drawn into the maze of confusion surrounding money. What we need to do is learn how to get a grip on our finances so that we will not fall prey to the patterns that will cause the fear, anxiety, frustration, and friction so often associated with personal finances. In this session we will focus on the three greatest threats to your personal financial freedom: the effect of deceitful advertising; the availability of easy credit; and the absence of disciplined budgeting practices. The goal will be to become free from the magnetic pull of finances so we can turn the attention of our lives to loving others and God with all our heart, soul, mind, and strength.

THE BIG PICTURE

Take time to read this introduction with the group. There are suggestions for how this can be done in the beginning of the leader's section.

A WIDE ANGLE VIEW

Question One Money can bring great joy and freedom. It can also cause despair and pain beyond description. Begin your group by describing how you have experienced both extremes of this spectrum.

A BIBLICAL PORTRAIT

Read 1 Timothy 6:6–10; Proverbs 30:8–9; Hebrews 13:5

Questions Two & Three The Bible is filled with teaching on
how to deal with personal finances. I once heard it said that
two-thirds of Jesus' parables have something to do with
money. Jesus' teachings on money inform us that there is a lot
more to life than the almighty dollar and what it can buy.
Jesus says some pretty strong stuff about people who are
obsessed with a desire to acquire more money; without apol-
ogy He calls them fools. It is foolish men and women who
pursue money and material things as a life goal.

The Bible says that money in the hands of the right people, if
it is handled the right way, can accomplish wonderful works
for God and others. Money can be used to feed the hungry,
clothe the naked, help the sick, support families, educate children, allow for travel, and expand opportunities, among other
good things. Money can be used to support widows and
orphans and advance the spreading of God's love through
kingdom activity.

But the Bible says that money in the hands of the wrong
people, people who mismanage money, can end up wreaking
havoc in our society. That type of money can stir up sins of
greed, oppression, envy, self-centeredness, inequity, and
injustice. That is why the Bible teaches that the love of money
is the starting point of all kinds of evil.

I've seen both sides of this, and so have you! I've seen people
who have their money in the proper perspective. They have
decided how much energy to invest in earning money and are
not addicted to earning it. I've seen followers of Christ learn
how to control money so that it doesn't control them. I've
seen them invest it wisely and share it generously. These
people seem to handle money and they live with freedom.
They have confidence and satisfaction with all of their financial affairs. They have a grip on their money, and this should
be the goal for each of our lives.

SHARPENING THE FOCUS

**Read Snapshot "Beware of the 'Permissible Lie'!"
before Question 4**

Questions Four & Five When it comes to advertising,
almost anything goes. Whole truths become half-truths. Reality becomes fantasy. Persuasion becomes manipulation. The
problem is that we are bombarded from all sides by these
campaigns. Every newspaper, magazine, billboard, neon sign,
radio, television program, and airport concourse we go down

blares out a message. Buy this, try this, travel here, believe our slogan, trust our promise. The sheer volume wears down our defenses.

Beyond the volume of this avalanche of advertisements is the effectiveness of some of them. They make us feel like *we have to buy*. I come home from a long day at work, sit down on one edge of the couch, and flip on the evening news. All of a sudden, I see a familiar restaurant ad. In living color I see a plate right in front of my face. I am already hungry when I see it . . . the green lettuce, yellow corn, a huge sizzling steak. Next to the luscious steak are crab legs, swimming in melted butter. A hand comes into the picture squeezing a lemon and the camera captures every crystal of lemon juice spurting all over the place. Without even thinking, I begin drooling. I find myself calling out to my wife, Lynne, "What's for dinner?" She says casually from the kitchen, "Lentil burgers and trail mix." Or at least that is the way it sounds as my eyes are still transfixed on the plate of food on the television. How can she compete with this carefully crafted image? Everything inside of me wants to say, "Let's go out tonight!" Have you ever been there?

I think the beer ads top them all. After watching a professional football game you end up feeling like a freak of nature if you don't drink beer. The advertisements hammer you, one after another. You start thinking, *I want to sit around the red-checked tablecloths and slap people on the back and share in the joy, laughter, and camaraderie that seems to always accompany throwing back a few cold ones*—at least in the commercials. If you watch enough beer ads, you end up thinking that real fellowship happens best in bars.

I was watching a football game with a recovering alcoholic once and after a big beer ad he muttered something to the effect, "They make hell look like heaven." I knew exactly what he meant. I would love to demand equal time from the beer companies. I would like them to show a family going through an intervention because Dad has just lost his job and beat up Mom again. Maybe we could hear a brief story told by a little girl who is growing up without a daddy because someone got drunk and decided they could drive themselves home. This is the part of the story we never see in slick advertisements.

Read Snapshot "I Want It All, and I Want It Now" before Question 6

Questions Six & Seven Proverbs 22:7 warns us about the lure of easy credit. It tells us that the borrower becomes the lender's slave. The concept of slavery can create vivid pictures in our minds. We think of those who are bound, trapped, and despairing, sensing they would never be free. That is exactly what it feels like when you get involved in easy credit and have to deal with large monthly payments. You are a slave. You feel trapped and bound. Suddenly you realize that even if you keep making the monthly payments, you will probably never get out of the trap.

You should never borrow on a depreciating item. This rules out almost everything, with the exception, perhaps, of real estate or a home. If you borrow for furniture, appliances, clothing, or anything that drops in value quickly, the minute you walk out of the store you have taken a beating. Now you're paying on something that is worth less and less. Above all else, beware of credit cards. Use them for identification purposes only. Pay everything in cash. Learn how to say no. You will never get a grip on your finances until you learn how to say no to easy credit.

Read Snapshot "When Spending Spins Out of Control" before Question 8

Question Eight Close your group with a time of truth-telling. Have group members finish one of the question's statements. Encourage other group members to respond if they have some perspective or wisdom to communicate.

PUTTING YOURSELF IN THE PICTURE

Challenge group members to take time in the coming week to use part or all of this application section as an opportunity for continued growth.

GETTING A GRIP ON YOUR SPIRITUAL LIFE

Hebrews 4:14–16; 10:19–25

INTRODUCTION

There are many motivating factors when it comes to attending church. There are also many motivations for growing in our spiritual lives. In this session, we will not focus primarily on church attendance, though this is certainly a key part of growing as followers of Christ. Instead, we will focus on how we approach the topic of spiritual growth. We will identify some of the pitfalls of the militaristic and libertarian approaches, and we will then focus on the value of a creative and dynamic approach to our spiritual lives that invites freedom and room for the Holy Spirit to work within us every moment of every day.

THE BIG PICTURE

Take time to read this introduction with the group. There are suggestions for how this can be done in the beginning of the leader's section.

A WIDE ANGLE VIEW

Question One Each person has their own set of reasons for attending worship. Although spiritual growth through corporate worship is not the primary focus of this session, this discussion will help group members get a pulse on what has motivated them toward spiritual growth in the past and what is motivating them now.

A BIBLICAL PORTRAIT

Read Hebrews 4:14–16; 10:19–25

Questions Two & Three It is human nature to feel unworthy in the presence of a perfect and holy God. Too many followers of Christ avoid intimacy with God because they feel unworthy. The good news of God is that He loves us even though we don't deserve it. Through Christ and His shed blood on the cross, the way to relationship with our heavenly Father has been opened.

We can draw near to the Father with boldness and confidence. Just think about it. The Maker of heaven and earth has thrown open His door and said, "Drop in any time!" When God extends an invitation, He means it. He wants us to connect with Him all through the day. He has opened the way so that we can experience the joy of a day-by-day, moment-by-moment relationship with Him.

SHARPENING THE FOCUS

Read Snapshot "The Militaristic Approach" before Question 4

Questions Four & Five When someone encourages a follower of Christ to adopt a militaristic approach to devotions, they are not giving an entirely bad idea. What they are suggesting is really a good thing. What can be wrong with reading the Bible and praying in a regular and disciplined way? As a matter of fact, biblical illiteracy is rampant throughout all Christendom. Some people have only a thimbleful of God's truth. They have never really learned the truth of God's Word. Reading your Bible expands your vistas of understanding of who God is and how faithful He has been throughout history. This is essential and imperative.

However, although this approach can be valuable, it is not the best approach. Even though there are some advantages to a rigorous, regimented, militaristic style of devotions, there are certainly some shortcomings. The first is that it has a tendency to compartmentalize your relationship with Christ. It's as though He intensely impacts about thirty minutes a day. After you have had your devotion, you get up from the table, put your Bible away, and go on with your day . . . business as usual.

Another concern about this approach is that it has a tendency to become mechanical, repetitious, and meaningless. The same old, same old can often lead to boredom.

This approach can also produce enormous amounts of guilt. If you don't keep up the regimen, you feel terrible. You have let down God and yourself! If this time feels dry or you miss a few days, you can feel like a real failure.

Now imagine keeping the regimen faithfully, day in and day out, so that you have it down to a pat routine. This can breed a poisonous form of spiritual pride. A group of Christians is sitting around the breakfast table and one guy says, "Well, this morning at 4:30, while I was having my devotional time . . ." and everyone around the table cringes. They feel bad that they are not as spiritual as him, and he feels great because of his disciplined spiritual exploits. Everyone looks at him and thinks, *Four-thirty, Wow! I barely made this meeting today, and this spiritual giant was up at four-thirty spending time with God!* The problem is, this is probably the exact reaction he was looking for. Pride has taken over.

Read Snapshot "The Libertarian Approach" before Question 6

Questions Six & Seven If I had to choose which extreme I would counsel people to take, I would encourage them to go on the militaristic side—at least it would help them develop consistent habits of Bible study and prayer. I have yet to meet a person with a libertarian attitude toward building a relationship with God who ever amounted to much spiritually. These folks rarely help others, they are sporadic in growth, and they almost never have a fire burning in their life. I don't see libertarians with a real zeal for God. They don't tend to experience great strides in building their relationship with Christ.

They have a tendency to let their relationship with Christ slide and watch their Bibles grow dusty. Their hearts get cold as they wait for the "feeling" to move them. Sadly, many of these people eventually fall away from the Lord.

Read Snapshot "The Creative-Relational Approach" before Question 8

Question Eight Most of us have had those wonderful times of feeling connected to God. In the middle of a busy schedule, we sense God's presence and love. Communication flows freely and the relationship is sweet. Tell some stories of these moments and celebrate how God reveals His presence in our lives.

Question Nine We all face things that act as roadblocks to intimacy with God. Identify where these exist in various areas of life. Identify the roadblocks and communicate ways you can remove these from your spiritual lives.

PUTTING YOURSELF IN THE PICTURE

Challenge group members to take time in the coming week to use part or all of this application section as an opportunity for continued growth.

GETTING A GRIP ON YOUR RELATIONSHIPS

Genesis 2:15–23; Psalm 133:1

INTRODUCTION

In this final session we will focus on the significance of relationships. It is critical that we establish strong ties with people who will positively influence our life. To a highly relational person who has many close friends, the richness of community is something they already experience. This session will be an affirmation and encouragement to go even deeper in their relationships. To the Lone Ranger types, the significance of relationships is still not clear. In this session we will focus on five reasons for pursuing strong, meaningful relationships. God made us to be in relationship, and we need to commit ourselves to get a grip on this essential element of a healthy life.

THE BIG PICTURE

Take time to read this introduction with the group. There are suggestions for how this can be done in the beginning of the leader's section.

A WIDE ANGLE VIEW

Question One Open your small group with a celebration of those people who mean a great deal to you. What do they add to your life, and what would you miss if they were gone?

When I think about the rich relationships I have, many memories flood my mind. I remember a time I went with some men from our church staff to Camp Paradise (our church camp). We spent a couple days shoveling snow off cabin roofs because we were concerned they might come crashing in due to the snow load. One night, as we sat exhausted around a fire in one of the cabins, we spent the evening counting our blessings. One of the guys said, sort of out of the blue, "I count this moment as one of my greatest blessings. Being with friends and experiencing rich relationships, that's real joy!" He said, "It is staggering for me to think that if I really needed transportation for two or three weeks, there are four or five people who would give me their car. If I needed a loan, I can think of four or five people who would give me a loan. If I needed help around my house for something, I could think of four or five people who would be there just at a phone call." He meant every word of it, and we all sat there with a deep sense that he was absolutely right.

A Biblical Portrait

Read Genesis 2:15–23; Psalm 133:1

Question Two God made us to be in relationship. When Adam was alone, God looked at the situation and said, "This is just not right. Something is missing from this picture." Until Adam was in relationship, things were not right. Once Adam and Eve were in relationship, things were "Very good!" From the very start, God's plan was community.

Question Three God's design for us is not simply relationships, but good, healthy relationships marked by unity. Take time as a group and reflect on what a relationship looks like when two people are experiencing unity. Paint a picture of what a relationship can look like when unity pervades the life of each person. Next, turn that coin over and discuss what marks a relationship that is filled with disunity. God's desire is for us to live together in unity. To know what this means, we need to have a picture of what unity and disunity look like.

Sharpening the Focus

Read Snapshot "Putting an End to Aloneness" before Question 4

Question Four We have all faced lonely times. Sometimes we can feel the deepest loneliness when we are surrounded by people! Allow time for group members to tell their stories. Also reflect on how deep and real relationships helped you through the lonely times.

Read Snapshot "Meaningful Relationships Multiply Our Joy" before Question 5

Question Five Joy is contagious. Just as we have all faced times of loneliness, we have also experienced the heights of joy. If relationships really do multiply joy, do some multiplication as a group and tell your stories of joy.

Read Snapshot "Meaningful Relationships Divide Our Sorrows" before Question 6

Question Six Some years ago my wife and I were leading a discipleship group. For the first six or eight months I had felt like I had to sell the idea of community to our group. We would do the lessons, pray together, do our memory work together, and study the Bible, but somehow it just felt like we were not connecting on a deep level. Then, a strange thing happened. One of the members of our group found out he had to have a serious surgery. The night before he had surgery our whole group got together and went to the hospital. We asked the nurse if we could have a little conference room and she gave permission. The ten of us sat around a little conference table and began to pray. Through this process, I could feel ten strangers becoming family. After everyone had prayed, the brother we were praying for wanted to pray, but he struggled. His struggle was not a fear of praying, but that he had been touched by community. Here were people he didn't really even know eight months before, yet who were all there, holding him up in prayer. This is dividing your sorrows. This is the joy of community.

Read Snapshot "Meaningful Relationships Afford Us Counsel" before Question 7

Question Seven The best way to experience the reality of how valuable counsel can be is to open the door to receive counsel. Take time as a group to communicate a specific area of life where you need the counsel of other Christ followers. Listen as other group members give you their perspective and wisdom.

Read Snapshot "Meaningful Relationships Create a Place for Accountability" before Question 8

Questions Eight & Nine Proverbs 27:17 says, "As iron sharpens iron, so one man sharpens another." We are called to sharpen the lives of our brothers and sisters. Do you know what would happen to your spiritual life, your business life, your financial life, or your physical life if you would give others full access? Dramatic change would be inevitable! You could not stop it.

It is time to say, "I want to be a godly man. I want to be a godly woman. I invite you into my life and I want you to hold me to the truth. I want you to coach me. I want you to confront me. I want you to cheer me on. I want you to tell me what I am doing right and what I am doing wrong. Show me how I could do it better. You pray for me and love me and I will do the same thing for you." If you would do that with just one brother or sister, there would be a radical transformation in your life.

PUTTING YOURSELF IN THE PICTURE

Challenge group members to take time in the coming week to use part or all of this application section as an opportunity for continued growth.

ADDITIONAL WILLOW CREEK RESOURCES

Small Group Resources

Leading Life-Changing Small Groups, by Bill Donahue and the Willow Creek Small Group Team

The Walking with God series, by Don Cousins and Judson Poling

Evangelism Resources

Becoming a Contagious Christian (book), by Bill Hybels and Mark Mittelberg

Becoming a Contagious Christian (training course), by Mark Mittelberg, Lee Strobel, and Bill Hybels

The Case for Christ, by Lee Strobel

God's Outrageous Claims, by Lee Strobel

Inside the Mind of Unchurched Harry and Mary, by Lee Strobel

Inside the Soul of a New Generation, by Tim Celek and Dieter Zander, with Patrick Kampert

The Journey: A Bible for Seeking God and Understanding Life

What Jesus Would Say, by Lee Strobel

Spiritual Gifts and Ministry

Network (training course), by Bruce Bugbee, Don Cousins, and Bill Hybels

What You Do Best, by Bruce Bugbee

Marriage and Parenting

Fit to Be Tied, by Bill and Lynne Hybels

Authenticity

Descending into Greatness, by Bill Hybels

Honest to God? by Bill Hybels

The Life You've Always Wanted, by John Ortberg

Love Beyond Reason, by John Ortberg

Ministry Resources

Christianity 101, by Gilbert Bilezikian

Rediscovering Church, by Bill and Lynne Hybels

The Source, compiled by Scott Dyer, introduction by Nancy Beach

Sunday Morning Live, edited by Steve Pederson

All of these resources are published in association with Zondervan Publishing House.

More Interactions

Authenticity: *Being Honest with God and Others:* 0-310-20674-X
Trade the mere trappings of Christianity for a vibrant faith that integrates Christian values into everyday life.

Commitment: *Developing Deeper Devotion to Christ:* 0-310-20683-9
Draw closer to Christ by learning the value of devotion to Him and recognizing what keeps people from enjoying His fellowship.

Community: *Building Relationships Within God's Family:* 0-310-20677-4
Find out how to move beyond superficial relationships and build lasting friendships.

Evangelism: *Becoming Stronger Salt and Brighter Light:* 0-310-20678-2
Discover the importance of sharing faith and learn the motivation and mindset behind evangelism.

Lessons on Love: *Following Christ's Example:* 0-310-20680-4
Develop a bold yet compassionate love by learning about various forms of love: from simple, everyday love to Christ's love, which transforms lives.

Marriage: *Building Real Intimacy:* 0-310-20675-8.
Recapture the thrill of marriage and also its lasting intimacy—the kind God designed for lovers to enjoy.

Parenthood: *Rising to the Challenge of a Lifetime:* 0-310-20676-6
See what the Bible says about one of the most important responsibilities of life, and gain insight from spouses, children, and other parents on how to successfully meet the challenge.

The Real You: *Discovering Your Identity in Christ:* 0-310-20682-0
Get a close-up view of the different roles God equips believers to play in His kingdom and sound biblical insights to help you fulfill them.

ZondervanPublishingHouse
Grand Rapids, Michigan

A *Division of* HarperCollins*Publishers*

Character: *Reclaiming Six Endangered Qualities:* 0-310-21716-4
Look at what can be done to strengthen "endangered" characteristics in one's life—courage, self-discipline, confidence, patience, contentment, and endurance.

Freedom: *Breaking the Chains that Bind You:* 0-310-21717-2
Discover how to overcome destructive habits and behaviors, whether it's anxiety, procrastination, weight issues, or depression, and find the freedom that is ours through Christ.

Fruit of the Spirit: *Living the Supernatural Life:* 0-310-21315-0
Take a close look at changing selfishness to selflessness. The six sessions cover how to develop the kind of character that bears the fruit of the spirit—love, joy, peace, patience, kindness, goodness, faithfulness, gentleness, and self-control.

Jesus: *Seeing Him More Clearly:* 0-310-21316-9
Focus on the big picture of who Jesus Christ is: a man, a great teacher, a physician, a servant, a good shepherd, and a king. Takes a close look at why He left heaven to live and die on earth.

Prayer: *Opening Your Heart to God:* 0-310-21714-8
Unlock the power of prayer and learn to effectively talk to God through personal prayer.

Psalms: *Deepening Your Relationship with God:* 0-310-21318-5
Examine the ways reading the psalms can help deepen your relationship with God, and let the message of the psalms capture your heart and fill you with expressions of gratitude, worship, and hope.

Transformation: *Letting God Change You from the Inside Out:* 0-310-21317-7
Learn to be more concerned with inner beauty—matters of the heart rather than outward appearances.

Transparency: *Discovering the Rewards of Truth-telling:* 0-310-21715-6
Examine your own level of truthfulness and receive advice on how to be truthful at all times in all relationships.

Look for Interactions *at your local Christian bookstore.*

Look to Willow Creek Resources®
The Life You've Always Wanted

John Ortberg
Foreword by Bill Hybels

"John Ortberg takes Jesus' call to abundant living seriously, joyfully, and realistically. He believes human transformation is genuinely possible, and he describes its process in sane and practical ways."
—Richard Foster, author, *Celebration of Discipline* **and** *Prayer: Finding the Heart's True Home*

Willow Creek teaching pastor John Ortberg calls us to the dynamic heartbeat of Christianity—God's power to bring change and growth—and shows us how we can attain it. Salvation without change was unheard-of among Christians of other days, he says, so why has the church today reduced faith to mere spiritual "fire insurance" that omits the best part of being a Christian?

As with a marathon runner, the secret of the Christian life lies not in trying harder, but in training consistently. *The Life You've Always Wanted* outlines seven spiritual disciplines and offers a road map toward true transformation, compelling because it starts out not with ourselves but with the object of our journey—Jesus Christ. Ortberg takes the spiritual disciplines out of the monastery and onto Main Street, and leads readers to transformation and true intimacy with God.

Hardcover: 0-310-21214-6
Softcover: 0-310-22699-6

Look for The Life You've Always Wanted *at your local bookstore.*

for a Deeper Spiritual Life

Christianity 101

Your Guide to Eight Basic Christian Beliefs
Gilbert Bilezikian

Part of developing a deeper devotion to Christ is developing an understanding of the basics of the Christian faith. But many Christians think
that the task of understanding the Bible and
Christian doctrine is beyond them. *Christianity
101* is for people who yearn to understand the
Christian faith, but who don't have a doctor-
ate in theology. Bilezikian presents eight
basic doctrines of Christianity—the Bible,
God, Christ, The Holy Spirit, Human
Beings, Redemption, The Church, and
The Last Things—in clear, simple lan-
guage that gives the seasoned Christian
a fresh understanding of the Bible and
its teachings and enables the new Christian to
become familiar with the ABCs of Christian doctrine.

Softcover: 0-310-55701-2

Look for Christianity 101 *at your local Christian bookstore.*

ZondervanPublishingHouse
Grand Rapids, Michigan

A Division of HarperCollins*Publishers*

WILLOW
CREEK

RESOURCES

WILLOW CREEK

RESOURCES

This resource was created to serve you.

It is just one of many ministry tools that are part of the Willow Creek Resources® line, published by the Willow Creek Association together with Zondervan Publishing House. The Willow Creek Association was created in 1992 to serve a rapidly growing number of churches from all across the denominational spectrum that are committed to helping unchurched people become fully devoted followers of Christ. There are now more than 2,500 WCA member churches worldwide.

The Willow Creek Association links like-minded leaders with each other and with strategic vision, information, and resources in order to build prevailing churches. Here are some of the ways it does that:

- **Church Leadership Conferences**—3 1/2-day events, held at Willow Creek Community Church in South Barrington, IL, that are being used by God to help church leaders find new and innovative ways to build prevailing churches that reach unchurched people.

- **The Leadership Summit**—a once-a-year event designed to increase the leadership effectiveness of pastors, ministry staff, volunteer church leaders, and Christians in business.

- **Willow Creek Resources®**—to provide churches with a trusted channel of ministry resources in areas of leadership, evangelism, spiritual gifts, small groups, drama, contemporary music, and more. For more information, call Willow Creek Resources® at 800/876-7335. Outside the US call 610/532-1249.

- *WCA News*—a bimonthly newsletter to inform you of the latest trends, resources, and information on WCA events from around the world.

- *The Exchange*—our classified ads publication to assist churches in recruiting key staff for ministry positions.

- **The Church Associates Directory**—to keep you in touch with other WCA member churches around the world.

- *WillowNet*—an Internet service that provides access to hundreds of Willow Creek messages, drama scripts, songs, videos, and multimedia suggestions. The system allows users to sort through these elements and download them for a fee.

- *Defining Moments*—a monthly audio journal for church leaders, in which Lee Strobel asks Bill Hybels and other Christian leaders probing questions to help you discover biblical principles and transferable strategies to help maximize your church's potential.

For conference and membership information please write or call:

Willow Creek Association   ph: (847) 765-0070
P.O. Box 3188   fax: (847) 765-5046
Barrington, IL 60011-3188   www.willowcreek.org